TEN KEYS TO
DYNAMIC CUSTOMER
RELATIONS

TEN KEYS TO DYNAMIC CUSTOMER RELATIONS

Gregory H Sorensen

KOGAN
PAGE

First published in the United States of America
in 1988 by Horizon Publishers & Distributors, Inc,
50 South 500 West, PO Box 490,
Bountiful, Utah 84010-0490

This edition first published in Great Britain in
1988 by Kogan Page Ltd, 120 Pentonville Road,
London N1 9JN

British Library Cataloguing in Publication Data

Sorensen, Gregory H.
  Ten keys to dynamic customer relations
  1 Companies. Customer services. Management
  aspects
  I. Title
  658.8'12

  ISBN 1-85091-791-4
  ISBN 1-85091-792-2 Pbk

Typeset by DP Photosetting, Aylesbury, Bucks
Printed and bound in Great Britain by
Dotesios Printers Ltd

Contents

Introduction

- Customers are fed up with the lack of attention to it.
- Businesses are apathetic or blind to it.
- Society is becoming more aware of it.
- Now is the time to address it.
- 'It' is *customer relations*.

Today's business environment is extremely competitive. Low pricing and product differentiation, for the most part, have lost their competitive edge. Soon, competition will be centred in the area of customer relations in many businesses.

This book discusses the need for effective customer relations and offers some practical suggestions for improvement. The application of these principles, coupled with sound management, will help a business not only to survive, but to prosper in the coming years. With practice, these principles can help you to increase your profitability and broaden your customer base.

CHAPTER 1

The Customer Pays Our Salaries!

For several months past, John had been concerned about declining sales. This was frustrating, because he could not pinpoint the problem.

It was not for lack of effort. John was a hard worker, arriving at work before his employees and usually leaving after they had gone.

John knew his business and the industry inside out. He had evaluated the 'important' areas of his business, yet was still unable to uncover the problem.

With the decrease in sales came a desperate need for more cash flow. His once untouched credit line was over-extended and he was acquiring more and larger liabilities.

In the past, John was able to identify a problem quickly and take the appropriate corrective action. But this was different. He could not even recognise the problem, let alone solve it.

The night before John was to meet his solicitor for some advice on the situation, he was unable to get much sleep. His mind was a whirlwind of thoughts and ideas. He was frustrated and despondent because of his inability to isolate the problem.

He arose before the alarm went off, got ready and went to work.

John's company was located near the city centre. He often cut through a hotel next to a car park. Such was the case this morning.

While walking down a hallway John approached an open conference room door. As he got closer, he could hear a loud voice ...

'A business can have good products, adequate financing, skilled managers, attractive decor, good location, and effective advertising campaigns ... and still fail.'

Surprised at the painful ring to the last two words, John stopped to listen. Glancing in, he could see that several people were assembled in a meeting. Not wanting to be obvious, he paused behind the open door.

'A business cannot be successful without happy and satisfied customers.'

It seemed to John that the books he'd read and the seminars he'd attended would lead one to believe that if the basic areas first mentioned by the man were solid, a business would be successful. Yet here was another element he hadn't really considered.

The man's statement hit John with great force. 'That could be the problem with my business,' he thought. 'Now that I think about it, we haven't treated our customers with the same care and concern that we did when we first opened the business. I've given so much attention to quality, productivity, finance, etc., that I've overlooked the area of customer relations. How could I neglect such a simple and vital principle?'

Then he remembered what someone had told him many years ago. 'Some businesses spend so much time and energy refining other disciplines such as accounting procedures, productivity and management style, that they overlook one of the most basic principles of all, effective customer relations. Too often, companies forget the hand that feeds them. It is a principle *often preached, but rarely practised.*'

John continued to listen to the conversation through the doorway. 'Though we're doing well, I think there's room for improvement. I don't ever want us to be guilty of getting caught up in other aspects of our business at the expense of ignoring customer relations. Good customer service is critical to our success today, as well as in the years to come.

'I've tried to put myself in your position. I realise work is not your only concern in life. Perhaps at times you feel that we expect too much. It occurred to me that it might help if you understood the "big picture." Why not let me help you understand management's point of view?'

Continuing, the man said, 'Let's talk about some trends. During the past many years, we've had a steady growth in sales, volume, and profits. When I started this business 27 years ago, the business environment was healthy. The economy was in an expansion mode and inflation was almost non-existent. Almost everyone had a job. People spent money on whatever tickled their fancy and there wasn't much competition. In fact, there were only a handful of companies in our entire industry. There were so many customers per business unit, it didn't seem to matter how we treated them, because we knew there were plenty more where they came from.

'Those were times of prosperity and growth. Obviously they're long gone!

'Now let's look at the present. What are some characteristics of today?'

An older gentleman raised his hand and said, 'There's a lot of competition.'

'Competition!' chaffed another, 'That's an understatement!'

The man probed further, 'What about competition?'

'Well,' the gentleman said, 'in our industry there are between ten and fifteen companies providing the same products that we do. The market can realistically handle only about half that many. There's a large number of companies competing for the enormous consumer market. Competition has driven prices way down, even compared to just a few years ago. It's amazing any of us can stay in business.'

The speaker jumped in, 'And it's not getting any better. From a numbers point of view, there's a substantially smaller number of cutomers per business unit. The so-called "endless" pool of customers is drying up.'

'What about the economy?'

'Not so wonderful!' a younger executive answered.

Another backed him up, adding, 'The whole economy seems very tight. People aren't all that free with their money.

'Inflation has slowed down, but this is in no way a booming economy.'

'Productivity,' the speaker said, resuming control of the conversation, 'is another key issue today. As you're well aware, higher costs and increased competition necessitate getting more productivity out of fewer employees.

'How good is customer service in most businesses today?'

'Pretty poor!' volunteered one woman. 'For example, I was in a shop a few nights ago and had to wait ten minutes at the counter before anyone helped me. And when an assistant finally came, she acted as though she were doing me a big favour by serving me. I was really irritated when I walked out of there.'

'Anyone else?' he asked.

Another woman answered, 'I was unhappy about the way I was treated at a grocer's a couple of days ago. The cashier never even looked at me. She grabbed my money and practically threw the change into my hand. And there I was, left with two small children and six bags of groceries to haul to the car. She never did thank me for my business. It'll be a long time before I shop there again.'

Several other people volunteered experiences, telling of a grumpy cashier, a telephone operator answering in a short and curt way, and not receiving so much as a 'thank you!' for having purchased a product from a business. The participants were beginning to get carried away with their complaints. It seemed as if everyone was well aware of the problem of poor customer service. They were apparently trying to release some of their frustrations.

Before things got out of control, the speaker took charge once again. 'All right, I was just trying to make a point, not start a riot. The point is that poor customer service seems to be the general rule, not an exception.' His employees nodded in agreement. 'I would venture to say that if you ask the management and employees at those companies where you received poor service how important customer service was, they would probably all say it was vital. Most businesses talk about how important good customer service is, but few follow through with appropriate actions.'

The man continued, 'I talked to the owner of a restaurant a couple of weeks ago. I asked him what he thought about customer relations. He replied that serving the customer was vital to his business, that in his restaurant, the customer was the king. The interesting point is that this was the same restaurant where I ate lunch last week. As it turns out, the service was poor, my meal was cold by the time it got to me, and I waited forever to get my bill. On top of that, when I went to pay for the meal, the manager asked if everything was all right. So I told him of the poor service and the cold meal. His reply was a quick, "Sorry sir," as he reached for the next customer's payment.

'Notice how the owner stressed the importance of good customer service, but when it came down to the service given to *his* customers, it was very poor. As it turns out, many companies fail to recognise the poor service their customers actually receive. Hence the importance of customer relations and why we're talking about it again today.

'So today we have a tight economy, an increasing number of businesses competing for a fairly constant number of customers, stiff competition, competitors driving prices down while the costs of producing those goods increases, smaller profits, and the need for increased productivity. And ironically, amid all of these challenging items, customer service is deplorable.

'So far as the economy in the future is concerned,' the speaker continued, 'who knows? I don't think there's an economist around who can say with any degree of certainty exactly what the future economic outlook is. People are more cautious these days, and I think they'll continue to be cautious about spending their hard-earned money.

'Products and services will probably become more similar in style and price. A customer will be able to get very similar products or services from several different businesses. Product differentiation will become increasingly more difficult.

'So the number of business start-ups will probably increase each year. Remember, the entrepreneur is a growing breed. It's becoming easier to start a business. Franchising makes it possible to set someone up with the necessary materials and knowledge of a specific market niche. Almost overnight, people can be trained and open for business. Entrances and exits, within many markets, are simple and common occurrences.

'This means there will be even fewer customers per business

unit. In other words, the size of the pie is staying pretty much the same, but the pieces continue to get smaller and smaller.

'All this means that competition will be stiffer than ever before. It will literally be "survival of the fittest." The companies that survive will be those who know their business, their industry, *and their customers*, and who treat their customers like gold.

'Perhaps the biggest change in the future,' the man continued, 'will be in the area of customer relations. Our society is becoming a high-tech and information-orientated society. The very nature of high tech results in a lack of human interaction. This trend is directly opposite to one of our most basic human needs, that of recognition. Thus, our need for human contact and recognition will become a more intense need in the years ahead.

'As a society, we desire the benefits of a high tech world. Yet as individuals, we have a tremendous need to be treated like individuals with feelings and emotions. We want the "human touch." Technology may come and go, but our *need for recognition and the human touch* will forever be a part of us.

'In the future, companies that *fill the needs of their customers, and treat those customers with respect, individuality, and personal attention*, will be successful and profitable.

'It's so vital for us to understand customers and their behaviour that perhaps we should back track a little and ask a couple of questions such as, what is a customer? And, do all organisations have customers?'

No one responded, perhaps because they appeared to be such simple questions. However, the speaker persisted with silence until the employees realised they were not going on until someone answered his questions.

'A customer,' replied an older man, 'is someone who buys a product or service from a business.'

The speaker asked the man, 'Do you have to buy a product to be a customer?'

He thought for a moment, then responded, 'I daresay not. I'd consider myself a customer of the government when I go to license my car. A college student is a customer of a university.' Pausing, he continued, 'I'd like to broaden my definition to someone who is the recipient of a product or service, be it a profit, non-profit, government or even a religious organisation. And in answer to your other question, I can't think of an organisation that wouldn't have customers.'

'I can't either,' replied the speaker. 'I'd think all organisations have customers in one form or another. But I'd like to add one thing more to your definition. I don't think a person must necessarily be limited to being the recipient of a product or service to be considered a customer. Someone who is merely seeking information is also considered a customer in my mind, regardless of whether he actually buys the product. For example, I went to the DIY store just to get some paint. I didn't buy anything at the time, I was just seeking information. They satisfied my need for information, so in that light I'd consider myself a customer.

'So, if all businesses and organisations have customers or potential customers' (the man held up one fist to signify the customer), 'and several companies have very similar products or services at comparable prices' (he held up the other fist to represent the companies), 'what is it that bridges the gap between the company's product and the customer, thus facilitating the transaction?'

'Advertising!' responded a younger man.

'Yes, that's true,' the man said, 'but what happens when the sale is over? It seems to me that advertising is at best one of a series of short-term bridges that need to be built on a regular basis.'

'Lower prices!' said another.

'True, lower prices do draw people in. Low pricing is something that any business can do to get customers into the store. It also means lower profits, and unless your costs are much less than your competition, a business that relies solely on low pricing won't have much long-term staying power. Low margins require high volume to make a profit. And with the pieces of the pie shrinking, a strategy of low pricing alone is very difficult. That also seems to be a short-term bridge that the competition could easily blow sky high with similar low pricing. And in the end, we'd all lose.'

'Immediate delivery!'

'Could be,' said the speaker. 'It would draw a certain number of people in. But what about those who are in no rush? Remember, people are very cautious, and they're generally willing to wait for the right deal.'

The group got tired of guessing, so the man said, 'These things are all important and even necessary at times. A successful business will have a good mix of what you've mentioned. But what I'm looking for is a long-term solution.' (He paced back and forth for a few moments.) 'I believe *effective customer relations* can bridge that gap for the long haul. Effective and efficient customer service can be the link, that *"golden link"*, that sets you apart from your competition. It may possibly be the *only* way to differentiate a business from its competition today and, more significantly, in the years to come.

'A business can no longer afford to treat its customers with passive complacency. A business does not do the customer a favour by serving him.

'Listen to this:

A CUSTOMER is the most important person ever in this office, in person or by post.

A CUSTOMER is not dependent on us, we are dependent on him.

A CUSTOMER is not an interruption to our work – he is the purpose of it. We are not doing him a favour by serving him, he is doing us a favour by giving us the opportunity to do so.

A CUSTOMER is not an outsider to our business, he is part of it.

A CUSTOMER is not a cold statistic, he is a flesh-and-blood human being with feelings and emotions like our own, and with biases and prejudices.

A CUSTOMER is not someone to argue or match wits with. Nobody ever wins an argument with a customer.

A CUSTOMER is a person who brings us his wants. It is our job to handle them in a manner profitable to him and to ourselves.

The Moral of the Story ...

THE CUSTOMER PAYS OUR SALARIES!

(Author Unknown)

'That's the bottom line. The customer is the boss. He pays our salaries!

'Does anyone disagree?' No one spoke up, so the man continued, 'This morning we've looked at the trends of business and their customers, defined what a customer is, and pointed out how we can think of the customer as our boss. Now let's look at how we can be more effective in the area of customer relations. Why don't we ...'

Just then someone closed the door, ending John's lesson on customer relations. Acting as if he wasn't listening to the meeting, he paused and pondered what he'd heard for a few minutes. He then headed for work, a little frustrated at not being able to hear more on the vital area of customer relations.

Rule 1
Never overlook or underestimate the importance of effective customer relations

Important points
1. A company can perform many business functions well and still not excel if it neglects the customer.
2. Good customer relations is often preached but rarely practised.
3. We all yearn for individual recognition and the human touch in our relations with others.
4. Effective customer relations is the *golden link* between a company with a good product and potential buyers.
5. For future success, companies must know their business and their industry well, effectively fill the needs of their customers, and *treat their customers with respect, individuality, and personal attention.*
6. A customer is someone who is seeking information or obtains a product or service from any organisation.
7. The customer is the boss.

CHAPTER 2
The Customer is Always Right!

John was relieved to have finally pinpointed the problem which was troubling his business. He was also very surprised at how he could have overlooked such a simple yet vital area as customer relations.

In the early years, customer relations had been a number one priority for his firm. Now he was embarrassed as he realised how this priority had slipped. He couldn't even remember the last time he gave any thought to pleasing his customers.

Unfortunately, what he could remember was an instance when an employee had offended a customer. He had tried to force his opinion on the customer. John had observed the interaction but didn't say anything because he was too busy with the new accounting software package. The customer was obviously frustrated and finally stormed out of the shop.

As John thought of this experience and the importance of treating customers properly, he remembered a principle that was once an explicit rule in his business, *the customer is always right!* 'Talk about slipping,' he thought, 'we're about as far from that rule as you can get.'

Early in his career, when he was a shop assistant, John had an experience that quickly taught him the importance of the customer always being right. He sat back in his chair and remembered the day when Mike, a departmental manager, had reiterated the importance of this principle.

'Perception! Perception! Perception!' Mike had said. 'When there is a problem, the customer doesn't care about our opinions or our perception. He doesn't care how much we may or may not know about a particular product. What matters is what the *customer perceives* the problem to be!

'It doesn't matter what the problem is in reality. It doesn't matter what you think the problem is. It doesn't matter what I think the problem is. What does matter is what the customer thinks the problem is! You need to be aware of the *customer's* perception. *It's the customer's perception you must deal with, not whether the machine works or not.*'

'But I knew for a fact,' said John, 'that the machine was in perfect working order. I tested it myself before I sold it to the customer. Even after he brought it back, I tested it again, and it still worked well.'

'I believe you,' Mike replied.

'Then why did you stop me from trying to convince him that it wasn't the machine's problem? That he simply wasn't using it right?'

Mike could see frustration written all over John's face and knew he had to go back a couple of steps. He said, 'John, let's ask some "What ifs?" Forget about the machine working properly, or not working for a moment. What would happen if you had continued to tell the gentleman that the machine was in perfect working order, that there was absolutely nothing wrong with it, and that he was not using it correctly? What if you didn't budge one inch?'

'Well,' said John, 'if I couldn't have convinced him that it wasn't the machine's fault, I would have had to tell him nicely that we simply couldn't do anything to help him.'

'Okay, so if the customer had realised nothing was going to happen, he'd have taken the machine back and left. Who would have won? And, who would have lost?'

'I don't really like the word lose, but I would have won. I mean we would have won, the shop. We wouldn't have had to take the machine back or repack it.' Proudly John continued, 'I would have saved the shop some money.'

'I appreciate your interest in helping the shop cut costs. But let me ask you another question. How do you think that man would have felt as he walked out of the shop?'

'I don't know. I daresay he would have felt a little silly for not being able to operate the machine properly.'

'That's right!' said Mike. 'Do you think he would have walked out of here with a bigger or a smaller ego?'

'Probably smaller.'

'You're right. What do you think the chances are that he would come back and risk feeling stupid or risk having his ego hurt again in a different situation?'

'Not very good,' replied John.

'Okay. Let me ask you another question. Roughly what percentage of our sales comes from repeat customers?'

'Well, I've heard you say in several meetings that 70 to 80 per cent of our sales come from repeat customers.'

'Right! Now again, in the "What if" situation, who would have *really* won? And who would have lost?'

'I don't think anyone would have won. We would both have lost.'

'That's correct!' said Mike. 'We would have sacrificed short-term gains at the expense of long-term benefits. The chances are that he would never have set foot inside our shop again. As if that weren't bad enough, he would most probably have spread the word about how difficult we were to do business with. That would have been two points against us. It would most definitely have been a lose-lose situation.

'On the other hand, if after *briefly* attempting to see if the machine wasn't working, and at the same time being *very* sensitive to the gentleman's perception of what the problem was, and realising that he was sure it was the machine's problem, you had cheerfully responded, "No problem sir, would you like me to exchange this for the same model or would you like a different type of machine?" and if you had then exchanged it for the desired machine and given a *more thorough* demonstration on how to operate it properly, then who would have won?'

Smiling with this new-found knowledge, John answered, 'We both would have won! We might have lost a little money in the short term, but that's nothing compared to the money we'd make for years to come from his loyalty.'

'That's right,' Mike responded. 'That would be a win-win

situation where both parties would be happy. I'd even wager that we would not lose any money, even up front. You see, that gentleman would leave here with a great ego, feeling good about himself, and very pleased with our business. There would be a good chance that he'd spread the word about how good we are to work with. That potential problem would be turned into a situation where we would most probably get new business from his friends. The bottom line is that we would make money, even when it appeared we might lose a little, all because of new business via his referrals.

'John, can you see why you're dealing more with the customer's perception than with the product itself? And how simple, inexpensive, and profitable it is to treat the customer correctly the first time?'

'I certainly can.'

'Just remember,' said Mike, 'that there are *never* two egos involved when dealing with customers. There is only one, and that is the customer's ego. *The customer is always right!* – even if you have a perfect knowledge that he's wrong. Customers don't like to admit they're wrong, nor do they have to. If they're made to look foolish, they will simply do their shopping elsewhere.'

John had learned a lot about dealing with customers from Mike. Now, years later, he still felt disappointed about any situation in which an employee offended a customer. In this instance, the employee argued with a customer over a product's capabilities. The customer was irate and stormed out of the door. John overheard the sales manager enquire as to what the problem was. The employee related what had transpired and the manager supported his actions saying, 'The product did all it was supposed to do. We can't help it if the customer wasn't happy. After all, there're always more where he came from.'

Shaking his head, John couldn't believe that he let something like that happen right under his nose. 'No wonder sales have been slipping,' he commented to himself.

Rule 2
The Customer is Always Right!

Important points

1. An employee must deal more with the customer's perception of a product or service than with the product itself.
2. The ego to be protected in an employee/customer relationship is the customer's.
3. Seek to have a win-win situation with each customer.
4. If the customer is always right, both the company and the customer win.
5. The concept that 'the customer is always right' deals with ego relationships. It does not mean that essential company rules and policies are violated to protect a customer's ego.
6. Customer adherence to company policies may require tactful presentation of these policies so that he will perceive that they are the 'basic rules of doing business' which govern both the company's employees and its customers in their relationships.

CHAPTER 3
A Positive Attitude Makes the Difference

Looking at his watch, John realised it was time to leave for his appointment. He wanted to leave early enough to get breakfast on the way.

His mind was preoccupied with the importance of customer relations. As he sat in the restaurant waiting to be served, he thought about his company and business in general, and how effective customer relations was an essential ingredient for the success of any business or organisation.

He saw a waitress coming towards him. She had spring in her step and was smiling from ear to ear. She looked him in the eye and greeted him with a big smile and an enthusiastic, 'Good morning sir! How are you today?'

'Very well thank you, and you?'

'Have you decided what you'd like to order or do you need a few moments more?' He told her he was ready and proceeded to give his order. She responded cheerfully, 'Thank you sir. Your order will be ready in a few minutes. Can I get anything for you in the meantime?'

'How about a cup of hot punch?'

Not sounding put out, but pleased to be of service the waitress said, 'It's not something we usually serve, but I'll be happy to see if I can find some for you.'

John was very impressed with the waitress. He appreciated her willingness to do something out of the ordinary. She could have politely said they didn't have punch on the menu, but she was willing to go out of her way to satisfy a customer's desires. That was impressive.

She actually appeared to love her job. As he compared her attitude to that of his employees, he thought it was too bad that everyone couldn't have the same excitement and enthusiasm about his job. There are many people who love their work; it's a shame that few ever show it.

A few minutes later, the waitress handed him a hot cup, commenting that she was able to find some punch and hoped it would be to his liking. Before leaving his table she asked, 'Is there anything else I can get for you, sir?'

John indicated there wasn't but asked if she wouldn't mind answering a question.

'Gladly,' she said.

Having courage from his recent experiences and a thirst to learn more, he said, 'Do you enjoy your work as much as you appear to?'

'Yes sir, I certainly do.'

'I don't mean to offend you. Its just that I'm so impressed with your attitude and how well you do your job I was wondering if you *really* loved your work or if you preferred to be doing something else and were simply making the best of the current situation. I don't work for your boss or anything like that. I'm just curious, that's all.'

The waitress thought for a moment, then replied, 'I finish work in a few minutes. Why don't I meet you out in front of the restaurant and I'll be happy to discuss it with you then.'

John finished his meal, paid the bill and met her in front by the bus stop.

'You asked if I really enjoyed my job or if I would prefer to do something else. To be honest, I have much higher hopes and ambitions. I'm going to night school so I can get a higher-paying job. I've got two kids to bring up and it takes more money than I can make here at the restaurant. You see, my husband passed away almost six months ago.'

'I'm sorry, I had no idea,' John said.

'Oh that's all right.'

'If you don't mind my asking, how do keep such a positive attitude while working at a job you don't really like, especially with the other things you're going through?'

'It's not easy. I really have to work at it sometimes. I suppose the most important thing is that I actually have a job, which is more than a lot of other people can say these days. I've got some wonderful children who depend on me. I'm healthy and there's really no good reason why I should mope around. Besides, you can always find someone else who's worse off than you. I just look on the positive side. I have to. It's the only way I can survive.

'A lot of times you simply have to *act* happy and enthusiastic, even when you don't feel that way. And do you know what? It's not long before you actually feel the way you've been acting. The old "act as if" principle really works.'

'Do you ever have a problem keeping a positive attitude towards customers?' asked John.

'As a matter of fact, I used to have a very poor attitude. I was indifferent to the customers. I was preoccupied with how picked-on I was and how rotten life had been to me. The last thing I thought of was what the customer thought of my attitude. I never gave any consideration to how I could make a customer's dining experience more enjoyable.'

'What caused the change of attitude?'

'Well, a couple of months after my husband died, I was having a really bad day. Everything that could go wrong, did. My kids were having a difficult time adjusting to living without their dad. There were some overdue funeral expenses, as well as a mountain of other unpaid bills. On top of that, I was doing badly in my evening class. It hit me all at once. Anyway, I wasn't smiling. I was short with the customers and I didn't really care about my job.

'Then something happened that changed my life. An older man pointed out in no uncertain terms that although he was sympathetic about people and their respective problems, when he came to our restaurant, he expected good food, good service, and not to be depressed because of an employee's bad attitude. He said when dealing with a customer, there is no legitimate reason for an employee to bring his problems into the work place. He said that customers are people like both of us who don't enjoy being around a moaner. He said a typical customer really doesn't care how bad a day an employee is having – he simply wants what he's paying for: a good product with good service.

'He told me I wasn't the only one with problems and that I ought to do myself a favour. If I am going to work, I should have a good time at it. And if I did so, two things would happen: I'd feel better about myself and have a brighter outlook on life, and also the customers would be very appreciative of an employee with a positive attitude.

'I couldn't believe someone would talk to me so bluntly until I found out that he was my boss's father who started the business years and years ago. At first I resented his saying those things, but after the shock wore off, I began to realise he was right. And ever since then, I've tried to forget my problems and put my best face forward. It's amazing how much more I enjoy the job I used to dislike. People really are fun to deal with, especially when I'm positive and enthusiastic.'

Looking at his watch, John realised he needed to leave. He complimented her again on doing a great job and thanked her for the insight she had shared. As he walked toward his car, he realised many of his employees had, over time, developed attitude problems. Most of his employees rarely smiled and enthusiasm was non-existent. His people didn't seem to be having any fun. And undoubtedly, customers were turned off by this attitude problem.

John thought about how much had been brought to his mind about customer relations in the past 24 hours. He could see he was gaining new insights concerning the problem he had been trying to solve for months.

Rule 3
Always be positive and enthusiastic!

Important points
1. Customers enjoy dealing with employees who smile. They also appreciate employees who are friendly and positive.
2. Always be willing to try to meet a customer's reasonable

request. Never appear 'put-out' by a customer's request, regardless of how common or uncommon it may be.

3. Realise the power and wisdom of sacrificing short-term benefits for long-term gains. One must learn to master 'small' things before one can master 'great' things.

4. A customer expects employees to leave their problems at home.

5. A customer really doesn't care how bad a day an employee has had.

6. Customers expect to get what they pay for: good products and good service.

7. Act positively and enthusiastically and you'll soon *be* positive and enthusiastic.

8. When an employee has a good attitude, his life as well as the customer's experience with a business will be more enjoyable and successful.

CHAPTER 4

Open and Honest Communication – The Vital Link

John got into his car and started to drive out of the car park. He only went a few feet before he realised he had a flat tyre. He looked at his watch and suddenly was very worried about getting to his appointment on time. At £60 an hour, he couldn't afford to keep his solicitor waiting. His appointment was in 25 minutes and at best it would take 15 minutes to get there. If he hurried, he could change the tyre and still be on time.

He took off his jacket and rolled up his sleeves. But as he opened the boot, his heart sank. There was no spare tyre. 'What happened to the spare tyre?' he thought. He got angry as he remembered that his son borrowed the car last weekend and had mentioned that he had a puncture that night. His son told him not to worry – he would get the tyre fixed the next day. He obviously didn't. John was furious!

He rushed back into the restaurant to call a taxi. John explained, 'It's very important that I get there by nine o'clock sharp. Can you have a taxi here within five minutes?'

'No problem,' said the girl on the switchboard.

'Are you sure? Because if you can't, I'll have to call another taxi.'

'No problem sir, there's a taxi in the area. I'll have him there in a few minutes.'

John waited impatiently as he watched two minutes tick by and no taxi came. He was getting more worried. He thought to himself, 'What if she couldn't locate the driver? What if he's late getting here?' He couldn't be late for his appointment, so he decided to call the taxi company again.

'I'm the person who just called. I wanted to make sure you were able to reach the taxi that was in the area.'

The girl replied curtly, 'He's on his way and should be there any time now.'

John paced back and forth, wondering what could take so long. He was getting more frustrated with each passing minute. Even if the taxi arrived now, he'd probably be late. This really irritated John. He called the taxi company again and said, 'Where is my taxi? It's been 10 minutes! You said the taxi would be here in plenty of time and it still isn't here. What's the problem?'

'I'm afraid you'll have to call another taxi company,' replied the girl in a dull and uncaring voice. 'We're short of drivers this morning.'

'WHAT!' shouted John angrily, 'You told me the driver was on his way over here. What happened to him?'

'There is a car in the area, but he's having some problems. They thought it would be fixed by now, but he's still not back on line.'

John was *livid*! He slammed the phone down, outraged at what had just happened.

Out of the corner of his eye, he saw a taxi drop someone off at an office a few doors down the street. He rushed over and asked the driver if he could take him to the city centre for an important appointment. The driver agreed and off they went, with John telling him to go faster. As the taxi screeched to a halt, John paid the driver and rushed into the building.

He hurried up to the receptionist, announced his name and said he had a nine o'clock appointment with Mr Jenkins. She told him to have a seat and they would call him in a few minutes. Relieved, John sank into a soft seat and picked up a magazine to pass the time. A few minutes later he looked at his watch; it was 9.20. He continued to wait.

At 9.45, he decided to go and find out what was going on. John approached the receptionist, who was now a different girl from the one who checked him in. They had switched about 10 minutes after John arrived. He said, 'Excuse me, my name is John Tyler. I've been here since nine o'clock waiting to see Mr Jenkins. Do you have any idea how much longer it will be?'

'I'm sorry sir,' replied the receptionist. 'Mr Jenkins was called out of town on business yesterday morning. Someone should have been in touch with you to reschedule your appointment.'

John couldn't believe what he was hearing. 'You must be joking!'

'I'm sorry, if you would like to see his secretary, she could set up another appointment for you.'

As John walked down the hall he wondered how anyone could be so inconsiderate. 'All they had to do was make a simple phone call. If I'd known, it wouldn't have bothered me. I would have simply rescheduled my other appointments. It is so inconsiderate!' He rescheduled his appointment for a week later.

As John thought about his experiences in terms of customer relations, his mind switched to his own business. He recalled several situations he was now ashamed of. He remembered when customers hadn't been properly informed; when they'd been told something when there was no way the commitment could be kept and situations where customers were left in the dark because of an employee's lack of consideration.

'Talk about poor customer relations,' John thought. He was now very impressed with how vital open and honest communication is in dealing with customers. After today's experiences, he'd learned that it doesn't matter so much when a product or service is promised, so long as the company keeps its commitment and delivers on time. People can wait longer than they anticipated, so long as they can plan on the goods when promised. If there is a problem, tell the customer the truth, even if it is bad news. NEVER, NEVER, NEVER lie or mislead a customer. Few things can sever a business/customer relationship faster than lying. The customer would much rather know the complete story. It is being promised one thing, only to receive another, that is so upsetting.

John also learned that communication must be open and honest at all times. Sometimes it only takes a simple phone call to inform a customer of a later development. Such a simple courtesy can have a profound effect on a customer's feelings towards a business. If only his solicitor had phoned him. It was the surprise, to say nothing of the inconvenience, of going all the way across town only to find out that his appointment had been cancelled.

And he was even more upset to realise that they had known several days previously that the cancellation would be necessary but had failed to contact him.

'The taxi company,' John thought, 'is a prime example of telling me one thing, either through exaggeration or deceit, and not being able to follow through with their promise. If they had been honest and told me they couldn't help me right then, I would have had time to call someone else. Then if the taxi company had offered their services at another time, I would most probably have called them when the need arose. As it is now, there's no way I'll ever use that company again. What's more, I'll do my best to see that no one else I know ever uses them either.'

John thought to himself as he was waiting for one of his employees to pick him up, 'I've really blown it with a lot of my most loyal customers. I'm sure they would have understood some of the problems we've been having had they been properly informed. A good customer realises there is the human element that occasionally goes awry. There are instances when there are delays and when there are problems which are beyond the control of a business. A customer can deal with what he has a knowledge of. *Often it's the lack of honest and open communication that breeds frustration, anger, disappointment, dissatisfaction, and the eventual loss of a customer.*'

Rule 4
Communication with customers must be open, honest, and timely!

Important points
1. Take time to communicate effectively with your customers.
2. Initiate communication with your customers; don't wait for them to come to you.
3. Use the phone effectively and regularly. A phone call is simple and can have a positive impact on customer relations.
4. Be considerate of the customer's time, money, efforts, and concerns.
5. Communicate freely at all times and discuss problems as they

arise. A customer can be understanding only when he is told everything that relates to his situation.

6. Never lie or mislead a customer!

CHAPTER 5
Satisfying Customers with Problem Solving

It was after five before John had his tyres repaired and got back to his office. He had so many feelings swelling up inside: frustration, anger and disappointment, but also a new surge of motivation. He had learned some important aspects of customer relations during the past few hours and was anxious to determine how he and his company could better serve their customers.

He went to the customer service department and began looking through the records. Picking up the merchandise return book, he read some of the reasons for returns. Incorrect size, wrong colour, too cumbersome – the list went on and on. There were pages and pages of returns. John knew that most companies had returns, but this was ridiculous.

John knew he couldn't blame anyone but himself. He was ultimately responsible for the success or failure of the business.

It had been a very long day and John was exhausted. He laid his head on the desk in disbelief, wondering how he could have gone so far astray from the principle that had been the impetus for the company's early success: that of effective customer relations. While resting, he remembered an instance that his wife, Judy, had had a few years ago when she was employed as a departmental manager at a local store.

One day Judy was helping one of her sales assistants, Sandra. Judy came over because a frustrated customer was ready to walk out. She introduced herself to the customer, 'Hello, my name is Judy. May I be of some assistance?'

'I hope so!' replied the customer. 'All I want is an inexpensive shirt.'

'No problem!' replied Judy. 'We have a very good selection right over here.'

As they walked over to the bargain section, the man declared, 'No! No! The other lady has already shown me those shirts. They're too cheap.'

Judy thought there might be a discrepancy in what the customer *said* he wanted and what he really wanted, so she began to probe. 'You indicated an interest in an inexpensive shirt, yet not a cheap shirt.'

'I'm just tired of buying a shirt and only being able to wear it five or six times before it looks worn out. I can't afford to keep replacing shirts like that.'

'So in the past, you were only able to wear your shirts five or six times before they looked too ragged, is that right?'

'That's right,' replied the customer.

'Have you ever worked out how much you've spent on shirts in a given year?'

'No.'

'So because of the low quality of shirts you've been buying, you've spent a lot of money on replacements. Is that so?

'Yes, that's right.'

'Ideally then, what do you really want in a shirt?'

'Ideally, I'd like a better-quality shirt, but I can't afford to spend more money.'

'So you want a better-quality shirt but don't feel you can afford it.' The customer nodded in agreement. 'If you don't mind, maybe I can point a few things out. Let's look at one shirt. And say that shirt is £12. Is that close to what you've been spending on shirts?'

'That's about right,' replied the customer.

'Over a three-year period, how many times would you have to replace that shirt?'

'At a guess, probably three or four times.'

'Let's take the best case and say you replaced it three times in three years. That would mean that over three years, you would spend at least £36. Is that right?'

'That's right.'

'Now suppose that you bought a shirt like this one.' Judy held up a good-quality shirt. 'My husband has several shirts just like this. He's been wearing them for three to four years and they still look good. They cost £25. So compared with our previous example, you would only need to buy one of these shirts. Do you see what I mean?'

'Yes I do.'

'So in the long run, buying lower-quality, less expensive shirts would cost about £36 compared to the £25 you'd spend if you bought a more expensive, high-quality shirt.'

'I've never thought of it like that before. I suppose what I really need is a couple of good-quality shirts – one in white and one in light blue if you have them.'

Judy proceeded to find the shirts the customer desired. As the customer was leaving he said, 'I really appreciate the time you spent with me. I finally feel I've got what I needed. I'll be back next week after I decide what other colours I want. I'll see you then!'

Sandra was very impressed with how Judy handled a customer who was very frustrated and turned him into a very satisfied customer. 'How did you know that what he was asking for was different from what he really wanted?'

'Before I answer your question, let me go back and ask you a couple of questions. When customers enter the store, what are their expectations?'

'I don't know,' replied Sandra, 'I suppose they're usually looking for a particular product.'

'Right. Is there ever a time when customers just want to ask some questions?'

'Oh certainly.'

'Why would they be looking for information or for a particular product?' asked Judy.

'Because that's what they want or need.'

'Exactly! They have a want or need and they simply want to fill that need. When customers come through those doors, they *expect us to help them satisfy a want, fill a need or solve a problem.* What do you think the customers expect of you as a salesperson?'

'I suppose they want me to help them fill their need.'

'Right! Customers expect you to help fill their need, either by giving information or by suggesting a particular product. Sometimes I'd like to get rid of the term "salesperson". If all our staff were good problem solvers, our sales would go through the roof, because if you help customers to solve a problem, the chances are very high that they will buy the product.

'This idea is not unique to our industry. People are hungry so they go to a restaurant. They crave sweets so they go to buy an ice cream. They need more clothes so they go to a clothes shop. They have a problem with an old car so they go to a car dealer. They have a potential problem of leaving their families in financial difficulties if they were to die unexpectedly so they go to an insurance broker.

'Customers simply expect to have their wants satisfied, their needs filled or problems solved.'

'I see what you mean,' said Sandra. 'It certainly makes a difference to look at things through the customer's eyes. It's an entirely different perspective. I used to think that we really had to push our products on to people to increase our sales. But now I see that sales will increase if I'm a good enough problem solver.'

'That's exactly right. Just bear in mind that people don't like to be sold. They like to buy. *People rarely have difficulty justifying a purchase if they're convinced it fills a need or solves a problem.* That's when the sale is easy. The difficulty comes when they don't have a clear understanding of their need.'

'So how can you tell if the need is not clear?'

'This goes back to your earlier question of how I knew that the customer wanted something different from what he was asking for. First of all, you need a clear understanding of the customer's need. Some customers come in and clearly state their needs. Those are the easy ones. The challenge and fun come when a customer says one thing but means another, like that man we just helped.'

'That wasn't my idea of fun,' said Sandra. 'I just kept getting more and more frustrated because he kept saying conflicting things. I had no idea what he really wanted.'

'And whose fault do you think that was?' Judy asked.

'His!' Sandra replied.

'Correction. It wasn't his fault. He obviously had a need or he wouldn't even be in the store. Yes, it's fine when a customer comes in and says "I need this specific thing or that specific item." The fact is that he does know what he wants. However, he may not be able to express it clearly enough for you to understand. You said yourself, *you* had no idea what he wanted.'

'But I asked him,' replied Sandra.

'That's a good start, but some of the time you need to probe further to help the customer understand more clearly what he wants. You weren't asking the right questions. Remember the last sales meeting when we discussed the importance of effective communication and the importance of posing probing questions and then listening carefully to uncover the customer's real needs? Sometimes that's the *only* way you'll ever understand the customer's needs well enough to satisfy them effectively. Do you remember the four signs of an unclear need?'

'Not off the top of my head. I'd have to refer to my notes.'

'The first one is the customer's use of conflicting terms. The last customer was a good example. He said he wanted an inexpensive shirt. But when we showed him an inexpensive shirt, he said it was too cheap. That was the clue which indicated that I needed to dig deeper.

'The second sign is when a customer hesitates about making a decision. This can signal one of two things. Either his need was not a strong need or the product didn't meet that need as well as he had hoped.'

'Wasn't the third one body language?' interrupted Sandra.

'That's right. This can include lack of eye contact, turning the body to the side when talking to you, nervous movements such as rocking back and forth on his feet, tapping his fingernails, clicking his pen, folded arms, and a myriad other nervous habits.

'The last and most obvious signal is a customer's inability to say exactly what he's looking for. This can be a rewarding opportunity for a salesperson. It can also take the most work. When you recognise one of these signals, then you may need to probe deeper to understand more clearly what the customer needs.'

'You certainly made it look easy.'

'It's almost second nature now, but it wasn't always that easy.

It took a lot of practice and hard work. Don't worry, just keep working at it.'

'By the way, why did you tell him that the delivery of spring colours would be here next Wednesday? I thought they were due in on Monday.'

'It's true the delivery is due here on Monday. But there are times when a delivery has been late. If I promised him that the goods would be here on Monday, and he came before they arrived, he might get upset or frustrated with our company. As it is, it was no problem for him to wait another couple of days. Even if the shipment is delayed, it should still be here when he does come in. Nothing makes customers more angry than when a company promises something and then is unable to keep that promise. Most customers are willing to wait longer for a product, so long as they can rely on what you promised. If you aren't sure about something, be honest and tell the customer that you aren't sure. Just be honest with them at all times. If a customer does insist, for example, on knowing exactly when we will be getting a particular product in, I try to give myself a 10 to 20 per cent buffer. I tell them a little longer than I would normally expect. Tell them what you *know* you can deliver, not just what you *think* you can deliver. It saves a lot of problems later on. Just remember to *make promises sparingly and keep them religiously!*'

'So if we understand the customers' expectations, come to a clear understanding of their need or problem, fill that need or solve that problem in a courteous and prompt fashion, and make promises sparingly and keep them religiously, what type of customers will we end up with?'

'Very satisfied customers,' replied Sandra. 'I now see why I make some customers so upset. I don't mean to, but I suppose that my optimism, coupled with thinking a customer has to have everything ASAP, more often than not gets me in hot water. Customers seem always to want their goods as soon as possible. I suppose they aren't always in as big a rush as I think they're in. I'm sure they would be more understanding if I told them the complete truth.'

'That's right!'

'I really was very impressed with your effort to make that

gentleman happy. Do you always go to that much trouble to make a customer satisfied?'

'Whenever possible, yes!' replied Judy. 'I'd really like to discuss this with you in detail, but I've got a meeting in a few minutes. Could I come back later on this afternoon and we'll discuss it more then?'

'Certainly. There's no rush, I was just curious, that's all.'

'I wish more of our assistants were as curious and concerned as you are,' said Judy. 'I'll be back in a little while.'

Rule 5
A customer is satisfied when his need has been filled or his problem solved in a courteous and timely fashion

Important points
1. A customer expects a business to fill his need or solve his problem.
2. The degree of customer satisfaction is contingent upon the match between the need and how well the product or service fills that need.
3. A customer expects courteous and prompt service at all times.
4. Customers don't like to be sold, they like to buy.
5. Customers find it easier to justify a purchase when they can see that it fills their need well.
6. To increase sales, concentrate on helping customers fill their needs or solve their problems.
7. A need can only be filled properly when it is clearly understood both by the customer and by the employee. It is the employee's responsibility to make the customer's need clear.
8. Four signs of an unclear need or want are:
   (a) a customer's inability to state clearly his need or want
   (b) a customer's use of conflicting terms
   (c) a customer's hesitation due to an unsatisfactory solution to the need or problem

    (d) any body language which indicates a customer is nervous about, or uncertain about, a particular decision.

9. Make promises sparingly and keep them religiously!
10. Communicate with the customer in terms of what you *know* rather than what you *think*.
11. Employees are expected to do anything within reason and within company policy to ensure customer satisfaction in a courteous and prompt manner.
12. Follow through on even the smallest detail. It is often attention to the smallest details that impresses customers the most.

CHAPTER 6
Building Customer Loyalty

John's memories of his wife's experience continued.

That afternoon Judy returned to where Sandra was working and said, 'It looks a little quiet this afternoon.'

'Unfortunately!' replied Sandra.

'Why don't we get Joan to come over and cover for you, so we can finish discussing the question you asked this morning.' As they walked to the employees' rest room, Judy said, 'This morning you seemed surprised that I would go to all that extra effort just to satisfy a customer.'

'To me, it seemed like overkill. You had already gone to a lot of effort just to uncover his real need.'

'Okay. If you were me, and you had found the white and blue shirts he had originally requested, and he asked if they came in pink, what would you have done?'

'Well,' replied Sandra, 'I'd look through the shirts in his size on the rack to see if I could find that colour.'

'And if you couldn't find a pink one?'

'Then I'd look up the style number in our catalogue to see if it was in fact available in pink.'

'So now you know that it comes in pink, what would you tell the customer?'

'That it does come in pink, but that we don't have it in stock. I'd suggest that he try one of our other stores or try again in a week or two, after the next shipment arrives.'

'All right,' responded Judy, 'let me ask you another question. What is customer loyalty?'

'It's when a customer comes back again and again.'

'And why would a customer want to come back?'

'Because he is a satisfied customer.'

'That's right. In other words, customer loyalty is a customer who is satisfied over some time. Sandra, what is it that makes a customer loyal to a particular company?'

'I suppose it's the products they sell.'

'So a customer is loyal to a company just because they have good products?'

'Oh no, the company also has to have good prices.'

'Good products at a fair price,' replied Judy. 'That's a good start. You've mentioned the first of four reasons why a customer is loyal.'

'So what are the other three?' asked Sandra.

'Well, one of the quickest ways to gain a customer's loyalty is to go out of your way to make him satisfied. Like this morning. I did spend a lot of time with that man. I went to a lot of extra effort to find out exactly when the pink shirt would be available in our store. Few things impress a customer more than when an employee bends over backwards to fill his needs. Often the result is a loyal customer. Have you ever gone to a company with a special situation or problem and simply asked if there was anything they could do to help you out, and then the company went to great lengths to solve your problem?'

'Yes,' Sandra replied, 'I did that just a few weeks ago, as a matter of fact.'

'What kind of feelings do you have towards that company?'

'They will always have my custom!'

'Exactly!' said Judy. 'Customers never forget when an employee goes out of his way to satisfy their needs. Those are usually the most loyal customers a company has. It seems that the more we have to work for a customer, the more loyal he is in return.

'The third characteristic that encourages loyalty is consistency. Many companies have built their businesses on that very principle. When a customer goes to such a business, there is no question as to whether he'll get what he pays for. Are there any companies you can think of that exemplify this principle?'

'There are some fast food restaurants and convenience stores that are extremely consistent.'

'The last principle,' said Judy, 'is doing a lot of "little" things for a customer. Do you know Sarah? She works a couple of departments over from you.'

'Yes I do.'

'She has a very loyal clientele. And I would venture to say that one of the main reasons why is that she pays attention to detail – the "little" things. She knows every one of her regular customers by name.'

'You're joking!'

'Every one. She has a system that helps her remember each name. She keeps a card for each customer. The card might include the name of his spouse, his occupation, how many kids they have, special interests, and his birthday. She sends each customer a birthday card, as well as a thank you card for each purchase.'

'That could get very expensive,' replied Sandra. 'I really wouldn't have the time, let alone the money, to do something like that.'

'I'm sure Sarah would tell you she can't afford not to spend the time and money to make sure she does everything possible to encourage customer loyalty. She's told me several times that it's actually very inexpensive compared to the returns she gets from such efforts. It's the extra little things she does that let her customers know she appreciates their business and values their relationship.

'So, when a customer's been satisfied on many different occasions, there's no reason why he would go anywhere else.'

The caretaker then closed a door so hard that it jolted John away from his memories of his wife's earlier experiences. As he began thinking of his own business once more, several recent experiences came to mind, such as when his salesman sold a product just to get the commission and to move on to the next customer, never giving a second thought to making sure the product would really fill the customer's needs, to say nothing of promises he freely gave but rarely kept.

John was too worn out to do any more productive thinking

that night. It was 9.30, so he decided to call it a day and head for home.

On the way, he thought about the principles he had learned about customer relations. It was ironic that the worse things got, the more likely it was for John to look for the problem in other more 'concrete' areas of his business.

Rule 6
A customer is loyal when, over time, he has received consistent, prompt and courteous service and products

Important points
1. Customer loyalty is encouraged by four principles:
   (a) Good products at fair prices.
   (b) Effort. The more you go out of your way, or the more work you do for a customer, the more loyal he tends to be to your company.
   (c) Consistency. It's essential that a customer receives excellent service every time he returns.
   (d) Attention to the 'little' things. The 'big' things count, but it's the little things that really make the difference.

CHAPTER 7

The Customer is King

John woke up the next morning with a new excitement and enthusiasm about restoring his company to profitability. He had indeed learned several valuable principles relating to customer relations.

John had always been impressed by a business owned by Tom, one of his good friends. Tom and his staff treated their customers well and the company was prospering. On his way to work, John stopped by to ask a question or two about their customer relations policy.

'John, it's good to see you,' said Tom. 'Come in and sit down.' After exchanging pleasantries Tom asked, 'What's on your mind, my friend?'

'Well, my business hasn't been going well for the past several months,' replied John.

'It's tough making an honest penny these days, isn't it?'

'It's more than that, Tom. You see, there are companies in my industry that are making bundles of money. And during the last couple of months, we've lost money. You don't know how hard I've tried to isolate the problem. I've looked at every aspect of the business, or so I thought. As it turns out, it seems that we've been neglecting the area of customer relations.'

'That sounds familiar,' responded Tom. 'I went through a similar thing five years ago.'

'How's that?'

'It happened a couple of years after we opened the business. When we started the company, we did a great job of treating our customers like kings. We almost worshipped the ground they walked on. I mean we would do *anything* within reason to make them happy and to make sure they were satisfied. Our business was constantly growing.

'Then a very subtle change of attitude occurred within our company. Gradually, we became more interested in profitability, productivity, procedures, and the practical aspects of running a business than we were in our customers. In our minds, our customers went from being our primary concern to near obscurity. I'm ashamed to admit it, but we were soon treating our customers as if they were in our way as we ran our business. We neglected the very hands that fed us. As you might guess, our sales dropped sharply. And at the time, I was baffled as to what the problem could have been. It was interesting, but the worse things became, the more I looked at finance, accounting, management style, advertising, and so forth, for a solution to the problem. I didn't have a clue what the problem was. Somehow, I simply overlooked customer relations.'

'So how did you turn it around?' asked John.

'Well, after I finally worked out that the problem was poor customer service, I called a company meeting. During that meeting I had one of my managers announce that' (he paused for a moment). 'Better still, tomorrow morning I have a meeting with a company I've been consulting on this very subject. They're having a company meeting and they are going to announce a new emphasis on customer relations. Why don't you come with me? I think you'll find it interesting. I'm sure they won't mind if you sit at the back with me and observe.'

'You're sure it would be all right?'

'I'll phone them right away if it would make you feel better.'

The next morning, John and Tom were sitting at the back of a large room filled with the company's employees. Gary, the general manager, called the meeting to order and said, 'I'm sure that most of you are well aware of the difficult times we've gone through recently. Because of the decrease in sales, we've needed to make some changes. These changes are for the good of the company.' Gary paused, then continued, 'Dick is no longer your boss.' The employees were all ears.

'Is he selling out?' asked one employee.

'Who's the new boss?' asked another.

'He's not selling out. Our new boss is waiting out in the hall. Our new boss is the very key to our future success. If we're attentive to his cares and concerns, we'll quickly return to being a profitable company. Let's give a warm welcome to our new boss, Mr Customer.' (Dick, disguised as a customer, entered the room.) He got some smiles, a few laughs, but most of the employees just looked puzzled.

'Perhaps I can explain why the customer is your new boss. Who decides the hours we're open?'

'You do, Dick,' replied an older lady.

'No, I set the hours because that's when the customer is most likely to come and do business with us. Who decides what products we carry and how many of each item we have in stock?

'Gary does,' answered one employee.

'Wrong again. Gary only orders what the customers want in terms of type and quantity.

'We could go on and on discussing various areas, and coming up with similar responses. Let me ask another question. Who pays your salaries?'

One employee tried to catch Dick out, 'You sign the cheques!'

'You're right, I do sign the cheques. But I certainly don't personally have enough money to pay your salaries. Where do you think the business gets its money?'

'From the customer,' responded several employees, catching on to Dick's train of thought.

John leaned over to Tom and said, 'This is a good way to get their attention. But how often do you think they'll have to remind the employees of the importance of serving the customer properly?

'Most employees really do want to do a good job. However, they, like you and me, need to be reminded periodically that the most important aspect of a business is the customer.'

In a serious tone, Dick continued, 'If you were expecting members of the Royal family to come and visit our company, what would you do to prepare? And, how would you act when they arrived?'

The eyes of one of the girls lit up as she said with excitement,

'That would be so exciting! We'd make sure that this place was spotless inside and out. Everything would be neat and tidy. Everything would be just so.'

'Would you do anything else?' asked Dick.

'We'd dress appropriately and our clothes would be clean and well pressed.'

'What about your product knowledge? Would you polish up on that as well?'

'Oh, of course!' replied an older employee. 'We wouldn't want to look like fools around someone like that.'

'What about your attitude?'

'We'd be cheerful, enthusiastic, and helpful,' answered a bubbly lady.

'That's easy to say now, but what if you were having a really bad day, or if you were simply in a rotten mood? Would you still be cheerful and enthusiastic?'

'Definitely!' replied the same lady. 'It wouldn't matter how bad a day you were having. With someone so important, you'd forget about your problems and concentrate on making sure the Royal family were treated … well, treated like kings. After all, how often would you have an opportunity like that?'

'I'm very impressed with the preparations you'd make and how you'd act. The reason I asked is because we have someone coming tomorrow, not unlike the Royal family in importance.'

The employees were all ears. They listened with anticipation as to who was coming.

Dick continued, 'Tomorrow's guests are more important to this business and its future than if the Queen herself were to come. I want you all to treat our honoured guests just as you said you'd treat Royalty. Tomorrow, the honoured guests are … (they all listened with bated breath) *our customers!*'

Their responses were gaining in enthusiasm. Dick went on to say, 'From now on, we are all going to be putting the customer first. Our customers are our guests, and we're going to treat them accordingly. We're going to treat every customer with the same attentiveness, courtesy, and respect that we'd show Royalty. If we don't, we'll all be out of a job very shortly. It's that simple.'

As John and Tom walked to the car, they commented on how common it is for companies to lose sight of the importance of good customer service. Tom re-emphasised the importance of putting the customer first *at all times*. 'After all,' he said, 'without customers, there wouldn't be a business.'

John thanked Tom for his time and was on his way. He thought, 'I haven't been this excited about going to work since the early days of my business.'

Rule 7
Treat each customer like Royalty!

Important points
1. Resist the tendency to shift emphasis from the customer to the day-to-day operations of running a business.
2. The more problems a company has, the more likely managers are to look at other 'important' aspects of a business, and overlook customer relations.
3. The customer decides the hours a company works and the products it sells.
4. A customer is the company's guest and should be treated accordingly. Always have a clean and orderly business. Make sure all employees have clean, pressed, and appropriate clothing.
5. Remember the obvious yet often overlooked fact, that without customers, there would be no business.

CHAPTER 8
Management's Responsibility

John was keen to implement the principles he had learned. He spent the morning planning the changes needed in his company's customer relations policy.

By mid-afternoon, John had prepared a list of things he expected from management. Since time was of the essence, he set up a meeting for later that afternoon.

After John had thanked the managers for staying after hours, he expressed his concern about the company's current situation. He related some of the things he had learned about customer relations and said he was confident that it was the weak link which was causing the decrease in sales. He told them he had a list of things that management could do to bring about a more effective and efficient customer relations policy.

'The current situation necessitates immediate action on our part,' said John. 'First of all, we must cure ourselves of something I'm going to refer to as "customer myopia".' John turned and wrote the term on the blackboard. 'Does anyone have an idea what I might mean by this term?'

'I'd guess it indicates a short-sighted view of a customer,' replied a senior manager.

'That's right! But why can short-sightedness in customer relations be so damaging to a business?'

"Now that you mention it,' said another manager, 'it seems that too many businesses care only about the here and now – about today's sales. They don't give much thought to the future. As long as money comes in today, they're happy.'

'Look what happened to the British car industry at the end of

World War 2,' suggested another. 'They could sell all they could produce, at home and abroad. And as long as the cars were selling, they had very little interest in customer needs. So when the industry, worldwide, woke up, first in Europe and then in Japan, the domestic car industry was badly hurt. They were left with cars that the public didn't want or need.'

'That's a perfect example,' said John. 'They wouldn't have had as many troubles if they had been more concerned with their customers' wants and needs. The customers' needs should have been a bigger part of their long-term planning. I'd like all of our long-term plans, decisions, and policies to indicate how they will relate to and affect our customers.'

'What is it that makes a business ignore its customers after they've served them so well in past years?' asked a senior manager.

'I think the main reason is a lack of focus. It's so easy to let other "more pressing" areas of a business get our attention. For example, what happens if finances are ignored and we write more cheques than we have funds to cover?'

'The bank calls us immediately,' said the accountant.

'And then what?' asked John.

'We remedy the problem PDQ!'

'Okay, what happens if a bottleneck stops a product from rolling off the production line?'

'We focus our attention on the problem immediately and solve it as soon as possible,' said the production manager.

'All right, what if an employee's work performance falls below an acceptable level?' asked John.

'We interview him to try and find out what the problem might be.'

'And when do you do these things?'

'As soon as the problem is recognised,' replied the personnel manager.

'These are just a few examples of some areas that receive our immediate attention when things aren't as they should be. But what happens when a customer doesn't receive good service?' There was complete silence. 'Does the customer demand better service at that very moment?' The managers shook their heads.

'Customers usually don't,' said John. 'Do they insist on talking to the management to air their concerns?' Again the managers shook their heads.

'They usually don't,' replied John. 'Do they give us a formal warning by telling us that we must treat them better or they will take their business elsewhere?' The managers still shook their heads. 'Then what happens when customers don't receive good service?'

'Usually they don't say anything – they just never return,' replied Jim.

'That's exactly right! It rarely comes to the attention of management. Very few customers will ever take the time or effort to make upper management aware of poor service. Customers will quietly go to another place of business. And if that isn't bad enough, they'll often tell others of the poor service they received at that particular business, while management continues to look in vain, as I did, at other areas of the business for a solution to the problem of decreasing sales. That's why I'd like us to consider all aspects of our business in terms of how they will affect our customers. Our first priority must be to serve the customer.'

'John, I think we should be very concerned about customer relations, but don't you think a manager's real effort needs to be focused on making sure the employees are committed to customer service? After all, they're the ones interacting with the customer.'

'So you think that customer service is really the responsibility of the front-line employee, is that right?'

'Yes.'

'Does anyone else agree with him?' Most of the other managers nodded in agreement.

'Wait a minute,' interrupted Jim, 'I strongly disagree! I think management must remain responsible for customer satisfaction.'

'How is that?' asked John.

'Ultimately, the responsibility for failure, as well as for success, lies with management. I agree, the front-line employees are the ones who actually interact with the customers. But it's our job to make sure they are properly trained and know how we expect them to treat the customer.'

I agree with Jim. If the employees don't treat our customers properly, it's partly our fault. If every employee innately knew how to treat customers with the respect, courtesy, and promptness they deserve, there would not be much need for a manager. We must do the training and clearly explain our expectations so the employees will have the skills and the motivation to serve our customers effectively.'

'I can see what you mean, John,' interrupted an older manager, 'but management is typically more dedicated than front-line employees. How are we going to put this notion across to the front-liners?'

'I think the best way to bring about a change of focus in our employees is for each of us to become more committed to putting the customer first. Most of the time, employees merely validate and justify their actions based on management's values, actions, and expectations. So, if management's first priority is customer relations, then the employee's first priority will likewise be customer relations.

'Let me ask another question. Is management's attitude toward the customer very important?'

'Yes it is,' replied a new manager.

'Why?' asked John.

'The customer can tell if management has a bad attitude towards customers, not only through their interaction with employees, but also through the overall workings of that department, from its personnel to its organisation. So eventually, the customer is, directly or indirectly, very aware of management's attitudes. Why is it so important for management to have a positive attitude?'

'We set the tone for how the employees act. As you just said, employees often validate their actions based on management's actions. I've noticed that when I'm having a bad day and I let it show, it's not long before the employees working around me are also a little down and melancholy.

'Have you ever come to work with a lot of enthusiasm and

positive talk?' He nodded his head. 'What happened to the mood of your employees?'

'They were positive and enthusiastic.'

'Over time,' said John, 'many of us have developed negative attitudes, and I'm probably the biggest offender. The customer can easily tell if we've got a bad attitude, and it's a turn off. If all the managers are positive and enthusiastic about all aspects of the business, our employees will probably be the same. And when we're all positive and enthusiastic, the customers will notice a healthy attitude and they'll feel happy about doing business with us.

'That's our goal. A loyal customer base is invaluable. It's built up consistently over a long period of time. And speaking of the long term, I'd like our company to broaden its scope. Let's get out of the frame of mind of merely selling a customer a product today. Let's *sell our customers in our company's ability to fill their needs or solve their problems in a consistent and prompt fashion today as well as in the years to come!*'

John wrote the words *physical and organisational structure* on the blackboard. He then asked, 'Why doesn't a figure skater wear cricket pads when he performs?'

'That's pretty obvious, isn't it,' observed a younger manager.

'I'd hope so, but answer it anyway if you wouldn't mind.'

'A skater needs to be graceful. He needs a lot of freedom in his movements. The cricket pads would obviously be too restrictive.'

'Good! Now, along those same lines, could the physical and organisational structure of a company also affect customer relations?'

With a confused look, the younger manager replied, 'I'm not sure that I know what you mean.'

'Let's say you were in a grocer's that only had two check-outs. Let's also say that you're ready to pay and there are 15 to 20 people in each line. How effective could their customer service be with two check-outs?'

'Not good.'

'Why not?'

'Regardless of how courteous they were to their customers,

the customers are bound to get upset and tired of waiting in such a long queue.'

'That's an extreme example of the physical structure of a business inhibiting effective customer relations. If a store had ten check-outs, but only had enough people to staff two of them and there were the same long queues, that would be an example of the organisational structure inhibiting good customer relations. Our physical and organisational structures need to facilitate, not inhibit, effective and efficient customer relations. Think about the best fast food restaurants. They are good examples of designing everything around the customer. They design the building to handle large groups of people very efficiently. And they usually have the necessary help during peak times to facilitate efficient customer flow. Their entire process focuses on serving the customer as efficiently and effectively as possible.'

'That's a good point,' replied the young manager. 'It certainly makes a lot of sense.'

'Over the next few days, we'll take a hard look at our physical layout and make the necessary improvements. We'll also look at our organisational structure. It may be that we'll switch some people around to make sure we have our people where they'll be most effective in helping our customers. We simply must make it pleasing and convenient for the customer to get the information he needs, find the product he desires, and check out quickly, thus leaving with a positive feeling about our company.'

After writing the next point on the board, John asked, 'How do you people feel about the *cleanliness* of our business?'

'Things aren't as clean as they used to be,' replied an older lady.

'As a customer, how do you feel when you go to a business that has dirty floors, shelves, or toilets?'

'Like not giving them my business,' replied the lady. 'There's been a few times when I've walked out of a restaurant just because their ladies' room was dirty.'

'It's just another part of making the customers feel comfortable in our shop. Not only will they feel more comfortable about doing business with us, but they'll be more likely to spend additional time shopping in a clean store. Jim, that's why ...'

'I'm one step ahead of you,' interrupted Jim. 'You'd like us to find another cleaning contractor, is that so?'

'That's right! I want this place to sparkle from the toilets to the front door. That might even mean doing some spot cleaning during the day as needed.'

'I'll take care of it,' said Jim.

John wrote the next item on the board: *paper flow*. 'How do you think paper flow could affect customer relations?'

'Our method of processing customers' orders,' replied Sue, 'can have a big effect on customer service.'

'Do you think you could streamline that process?'

'I'll do my best.'

'I'd like to cut out as many steps as possible, so that when a customer enquires about his order, we'll be able to give him more information in a shorter time. Some of the current technology might help in this area.'

'There's a lot of technology available. It might mean updating our old system or adding some new equipment,' replied Sue.

'If that's what it takes, we'll do it. Let's get all the mileage we can get from today's technology. To be honest, before my recent experiences, I thought technology existed to make management's job easier and more efficient. Now I tend to think of technology in the light of what it will do for the customer. Customer flow – from phone calls, orders, pick-ups, questions, etc. – could be streamlined for ease, effectiveness, and efficiency with the help of today's technology. Anyway, if you'd see what you can do, I'd appreciate it.'

'I certainly will,' replied Sue.

'There are lots of things we need to do to facilitate and streamline our physical and organisational structure, but let's just do these things to get started. We'll refine it later. Eventually I'd like us to look at *every* aspect that could have anything to do with serving the customer with greater effectiveness and efficiency – from the decor, to the paper flow, to the size of our shop, to customer parking, even temperature control. Eventually I'd like everything to reflect a passion for serving our customers.

'I want us to change our focus from simply getting the product out to that of serving the customer better. It's ironic, but *when the customer's needs are being met in the most effective and efficient way possible, productivity and profitability will follow!'*

'John, how do you plan to measure our effectiveness in customer service?'

'I'm glad you asked.' After John had written the next item on the board, he said, 'A *feedback system* is essential to a good customer relations policy. An effective feedback system will help us to monitor customer satisfaction. I haven't designed a system as yet. I'd like your input on the characteristics you feel such a system should have.'

'I think for a system to be worthwhile,' volunteered Jim, 'it must provide quickly the information we need. It wouldn't be much use to us if it took six months to get the information to management. By that time, we could go bust if there were a serious problem that went undetected.'

'Good! What else would be important?'

'The system ought to be simple,' added an older manager. 'If you want good participation from employees as well as customers, the simpler the better. I've worked for companies that have had elaborate systems and others that had simple ones. The simpler they are, the more participation you get. However, there is also a balance you need to maintain between being so simple that the information is worthless, and being so complex as to hinder participation.'

'All right, so we need to make it as simple as possible while still obtaining the necessary information. What else?' asked John.

'Whatever the system,' said another manager, 'it needs to provide honest feedback. Somehow we need to make sure that a customer would be absolutely honest if there was a problem.'

'That's a key item,' added a different manager. 'If a customer is not going to feel free to be open and honest about any problems or difficulties, then there is no use in spending the time or money to do any of this.'

'I agree,' said John. 'But that's easier said than done. Some people are not all that willing to bring up a problem.'

'What about the cost of such a programme?' a manager asked.

'That's another area where you need to keep a balance. We could have immediate feedback with all the information we needed, but it may cost thousands of pounds. That's why we need a trade-off between promptness, simplicity, and the amount of information obtained.

'I also feel it's very important to get customers back in the shop, especially if they've had a bad experience. All we can really ask for is a second chance.

'Now, let's try to think of some way that would motivate our customers to come back in the event of a problem. Anything else regarding the feedback system?' asked John. No one replied so he wrote the next item on the board.

'The next thing is that I would like management to *treat all employees fairly*. Why do you think this would have an impact on customer relations?'

'They're the ones on the front line actually interacting with the customers,' said Jim. 'And if they're not happy, or if they feel that management is not treating them right, they will most probably not treat customers with respect and consideration.'

'It's ironic,' John added, 'that those who are the least well paid, have the least experience in dealing with customers, and the least amount of time with the company, are the employees on the front line dealing with our customers. As important and vital as it is to treat our customers well and give them the service they deserve, you'd think that we'd put our best and most experienced people on the front line to deal with the customer.'

'How feasible would that be?' asked a concerned older lady.

'We all know that's not very feasible. But what could we do that might minimise that irony?'

'Well, in addition to treating the employees fairly, I think we should train them better,' said Jim.

'As far as I know, that's the only reasonable substitute for experience. I realise our employees receive extensive training on how to operate the cash register as well as some good information on product knowledge. We then expect them to know innately how to handle the customer in the most effective and courteous way possible. Does that sound as though we've been realistic in our expectations of our employees?'

'Putting it like that, no,' replied an older manager. 'In the near future, I want our training programme to give as much, if not more, time and effort to customer relations. The more I've thought about it, the more I realise how foolish we've been to think that someone off the street would naturally know how to treat a customer effectively, how to handle any problems a customer might have, and how to do the necessary probing to really understand what it is the customer needs. We can't afford to let our employees learn these things by trial and error. Our customers are too valuable. We must shorten the learning curve in the customer service area. And a thorough training pro- gramme is the best way I know to shorten that curve. Is the customer the only one who suffers in a difficult situation when an employee is not well trained?'

'There's no question that the customer gets frustrated, but it's frustrating for the employee too,' said a younger lady. 'Nobody likes being in a difficult situation.'

'That's right! So because an employee has not received the necessary training, when faced with a difficult situation, the customer is dissatisfied and frustrated, and also the employee becomes frustrated and defensive, often ending up offending the customer even more. We risk a loss of future revenue if the customer never returns.'

John continued, 'A prominent businessman told me many years ago, "If you are prepared, you have nothing to fear." With the proper training, our employees would have little reason to be afraid of even the most difficult situation that might arise when dealing with a customer.'

'Think of the confidence our employees would have,' added Jim. 'And that confidence is bound to be felt by the customer.'

'That's right!' said John. 'Anway, I'm convinced that a good customer relations training programme would be worth its weight in gold.'

Jim raised his hand. 'I think that in connection with a good training programme, there should be a good motivation pro- gramme too. Employees sometimes need an extra incentive to get them to perform well in a particular area.'

'I agree,' said John. 'Each of you needs to quantify or measure somehow the effectiveness and efficiency of your employees' customer relations skills. Then set some specific goals and rewards for accomplishing those goals. Let's face it, *what gets measured, gets results!'*

'What can we do to develop more teamwork within our company?' asked a departmental manager. 'What John is talking about could be broadened to include some programmes based on a department as a whole. I've seen some effective programmes that reward everyone within a particular department when the goal is met. Few things motivate like peer pressure.'

'Teamwork within our company could be improved,' said John. 'Customers don't think of us as individuals. They think that each employee "is" the company. When they think an employee has given them a raw deal, they think the whole company gave them a raw deal. That's why it would be so beneficial to develop a better team concept.'

John wrote the last item on the board. 'There's something that I will not tolerate any more, and that's *talking in front of the customer about things not related to the customer.* Do you know why this is so disturbing to customer relations?

'I don't know about anyone else, but it really bothers me when I go into a shop and overhear employees talking about some personal matter, especially when I'm waiting for service. It's totally unprofessional and leaves me with a very poor impression of that entire company.'

'I know what you mean,' added another manager. 'I've even heard employees in other shops talking in a negative way about other employees and their company.'

'Okay, so we all understand the importance of never having a personal conversation in front of a customer, *especially* when a customer is waiting for service! This also means no reproving, belittling, or joking about the company, its policies, or its personnel in front of a customer. We, as management, need to set the example for the rest of the employees in these matters.

'Anyway, from now on, we're going to treat our customers like *gold*, as if they are the most important part of our business, as if they are Royalty. You wouldn't get angry or reprimand an employee in front of a king. You wouldn't have a personal phone conversation with a friend while a king was waiting for help. You wouldn't ignore a king if he walked in the front door, be negative around him, or treat anything he asked of you in a light or uncaring manner. You would be grateful he came into your shop. You wouldn't sell him one thing knowing he needed another, or rudely brush him off just to get to the next customer. The bottom line is that from now on we're all going to treat our customers like Royalty.

'In conclusion, I want you all to know how glad I am that we're on the same team. I appreciate all the work you've done in the past, and I'm excited about what the future holds for us as we apply these principles. What's especially good about the things I've mentioned is that they're free. They simply take a bit more time and effort on our behalf. But the returns for our efforts will be phenomenal. They're so simple and inexpensive, it's sad that so many businesses dismiss them as unimportant and unnecessary.'

John was pleased with the reaction of the managers. He overheard one deparmental manager challenge another to obtain the highest level of customer satisfaction as they were leaving the conference room.

Rule 8
Management is ultimately responsible for effective and efficient customer relations

Important points

1. Management must rid itself of 'customer myopia'.
2. When making decisions and performing long-term planning, a primary concern should be how the changes will affect the customer.
3. Management must set the example by having positive and enthusiastic attitudes.
4. Don't just sell a product today, sell the customer on your company's ability to fill his needs in the years to come as well as today.
5. A company's physical and organisational structure must facilitate effective customer relations.
6. A feedback system is vital to help management monitor the

level of customer satisfaction. Several characteristics of such a system might include:

(a) providing information promptly
(b) simplicity
(c) providing honest feedback
(d) cost effectiveness
(e) motivation for customers to come back to the business if they were not satisfied or there was a problem.

7. Fair treatment of employees precipitates employees' effective and efficient treatment of customers.

8. Customer relations training should be an essential part of an employee's training programme.

9. A programme should be in place to motivate employees to achieve higher levels of customer satisfaction. Remember, what gets measured, gets results.

10. In the customer's presence, management and employees must only talk about items pertaining to a customer. No personal conversations or negative talk about personnel or the company should ever be tolerated.

11. A sound customer relations policy is very inexpensive to implement and the benefits can be tremendous.

CHAPTER 9
Six Steps to Effective Customer Relations

John realised that his employees needed a lot of training in how to serve their customers properly. After thinking about his experiences over the past few days, John came up with six steps to effective customer relations. He planned to present these steps at a company meeting the next day. That evening, John's son Keith proudly announced he'd got a job at a local departmental store and asked for some tricks of the trade that his father had learned through the years.

Flattered and proud to receive his son's request, John said, 'I've come up with six steps that should help you out.' His son leaned forward, eager in his enthusiasm to learn. John continued, 'The first step is the greeting. This is important for a couple of reasons. First of all, it sets the stage for the rest of the transaction. If it's positive, it puts both you and the customer in a good frame of mind. And it can facilitate good communication, which is vital for good customer service.'

'What if the greeting isn't positive?' asked Keith.

'If you start off on the wrong foot, you've got to do your best to turn it around. It's difficult, but not impossible.'

'So how do you turn it around?'

Be *very* polite and go out of your way to help that customer. If you said something that might have been misunderstood, then apologise. I was helping a customer this afternoon and we got off to a rocky start. For some reason, there was some friction between us. Now I realise that a person can't get along well with everyone, all the time. But I still try to make the best out of an awkward situation. Anyway, I noticed that this customer was wearing a watchstrap with a lot of elaborate metalwork and turquoise, so I commented on how nice it looked. The customer's face lit up as he told me where he got it, as well as the significance of several of the patterns. From then on, we got along very well. So if sincere, a compliment or even humour can help to turn a touchy situation around.

'Your greeting is also the customer's first impression of you. And that first impression is one of the things the customer will remember after he's left your store.'

'Why is that?' asked Keith.

'Remember a couple of days ago when you and I were out looking at stereos? After we left the first shop you said that salesman was an idiot.'

'Yes, I remember.'

'Why did you say he was an idiot?'

'I don't know why. He just seemed stupid.'

'He *seemed* like an idiot to you. The reason you didn't think much of him was most probably due to a negative first impression. It took only a few moments to form an impression, positive or negative. Your customers will be just as quick to judge you. Whether consciously or unconsciously, good or bad, nearly everyone is subject to first impressions. You can never make a second first impression. That's why it's essential to do all you can to make a customer's first impression positive.'

'What can you do to make sure it's positive?'

'Greet each customer with a big smile and a handshake if it's appropriate. I can't over-emphasise the importance of a simple smile. It's the universal sign of friendship and acceptance. A smile can make a customer feel welcome, that you really appreciate his coming to your shop.

'Also, whenever appropriate, introduce yourself to the customer. Offer your name, and then if you wait a moment, usually he will give you his. If he doesn't offer his name, you might simply ask for it. Nothing is more important to a person than the sound of his name. If you can get his name and then use it often during the transaction, you'll make him feel important.

'It's also a good idea to greet the customer as soon as possible. Even if you're still helping another customer, tell him you'll be with him as soon as you can. If you simply acknowledge his presence, a customer is more likely to be patient while waiting for your help.

'The next step is to develop a rapport. This is when you can recognise the customer's individuality. For example, you might comment on something that is unique to him. I remember an experience that your mother had the last time she was pregnant. She took her car in for a service and the attendant congratulated her on the impending arrival and asked when the baby was due. He then mentioned that his wife just had a little girl a few months before. Anyway, she commented on how good that made her feel and that she wanted to keep going there to have her car serviced.

'You could also comment on his bright children, smart car, beautiful ring, unique briefcase, etc. The recognition really makes him feel good and he'll immediately have positive feelings towards you and your company. This step could also be called the "feeling good" stage of the transaction. Some people use humour to generate good feelings.

'Good rapport opens the door even wider for more effective communication later on. It's also the beginning of a friendship that can develop as the transaction progresses.'

'How long should this step last?' asked Keith.

'Good question. Most often, it will only last a few minutes. However, the length of time for this, as well as the other steps, will vary depending on your role in the selling process as well as the type and price of the product you're dealing with. For example, a cashier doesn't have the time or the need to spend a lot of time developing a rapport. However, keep in mind that some people have a knack for developing trust and rapport in a short period of time. As the price and complexity of a product goes up, the time and effort should also increase. The level of trust needed to sell your particular product successfully can be a guide to how much time you should spend developing a rapport.

'The third step is the means by which customer satisfaction and loyalty are eventually achieved: assessing the customer's need.'

'Don't you just ask the customer what he wants?' asked Keith.

'Ideally, yes, but there are many times when the customer is not all that sure what he wants, or he may ask for something that really won't fill his need. That's why it's probably the most difficult step. *The ultimate success of the entire transaction is dependent on the mutually understood clarity of the customer's need.'*

'So how do you find out what the real need is when the customer doesn't come right out and tell you?'

'When the need isn't clear, you need to spend more time and effort in uncovering that need.' John then told the story of the man who asked for an 'inexpensive' shirt, but didn't want a 'cheap' one. He then continued, 'Asking a lot of questions without annoying the customer is a skill that needs to be developed.'

'That seems like a difficult thing to do.'

'It may seem overwhelming at first, but with some practice, it won't be long before you'll be a real professional.

'Anyway, the fourth step is to fill the customer's need. If you've discovered the customer's real need, this step is easy. Two things can happen – either you can fill the need or you can't. It's that simple.

'Let's say that you can fill the need. You then fill that need in a prompt and courteous fashion. Give them two or three alternatives along with their respective advantages and disadvantages. Be sure to take the time to educate your customers. They really appreciate it and it helps to minimise "buyer's remorse" that hits many customers after a purchase. If you've pointed out the pros and cons of each alternative, the customer will have greater confidence in his decison. Buyer's remorse will be minimised, and you'll end up with a *very* satisfied customer.'

'What if you can't fill his need?'

'First of all, if the product you need is out of stock, find out exactly when you'll be getting it back in. A word of caution – be extremely careful not to promise what you can't deliver. After you find out the delivery date, you should then offer to phone him when it comes in, or ask him to call back at the appropriate time.'

'What if you don't even stock the product?'

'Then you must be honest, right away, and say that you don't have that particular product. But also mention what you do have that might be used as a substitute, with its appropriate advantages and disadvantages.

'If he's still not satisfied, then you might suggest where he could find the product he needs.'

'Wouldn't my boss get upset if I suggested he go to a competitor to find the product?'

'There are a lot of people who think it's a foolish thing to do. I personally think that in most instances, it's a good idea. If you have done the previous steps correctly, the customer has gained confidence in you and you've both developed a friendship. If you tell him where he can go to find the product, you're still helping to fill his need. His need for information has been satisfied by you and he'll have confidence in your recommendations. So the customer will still be satisfied with the service you rendered, even if he goes elsewhere for the final purchase. You're much better off to tell him where to buy the product he needs and leave him satisfied because of your suggestion, than to sell him a product that does not fill his need.

'Because you were the one who helped him to understand his need and what product would best fill that need, the chances are good that he'll come back to you when another need comes up. So you will win in the long run, even though you might have lost a sale that day. When done properly, this step will make a customer truly satisfied. And that's what we're after. So, the fourth step is to fill the customer's need effectively.

'The fifth step is to ensure customer satisfaction.'

'What do you mean "ensure" satisfaction?' asked Keith.

'I mean make absolutely sure that the customer is satisfied, even when he leaves your shop. Ask him to come back if he has any problems with the product. In a way, it's a sort of insurance policy. If for any reason the previous steps weren't done properly, and the customer isn't satisfied, this step will allow you to redeem yourself. Make sure you keep the door open to remedy any problem or dissatisfaction that might arise. Be sincere in asking him to come back if he has any problems. In some instances, it can really save your neck.

'I recall purchasing a particular product. I was elated with the purchase, but the assistant sincerely asked me to come back if there were any problems. I commented that it was just what I wanted and there wouldn't be any reason to return. The assistant simply said that he hoped that was the case but to remember the door was always open. I felt like a fool, but when I got home, I realised that the product wasn't going to solve the particular problem. I felt stupid, but I went back and the man was really friendly and glad I came back to remedy the problem. Anyway, I left there feeling so good about that company that I've recommended them to all my friends.

'This step can go a long way in building customer loyalty because a customer is not only guaranteed satisfaction, but he knows that in the future he will most likely receive the same good treatment. So, naturally, the customer will return when he has a need, thus beginning the cycle that is so crucial in developing loyalty.

'The last step is when you invite the customer to come back. Just as the first impression is vital, the last words spoken often linger with a customer long after he has left your place of business. Be genuine, have a smile, and with enthusiasm thank him for his business and ask him to come back and see you soon. Without fail, genuinely thank him and invite him back.

'Some companies even go one step further. They bait the customer by announcing the arrival of, for example, the new spring line, or some other item that might be of interest to him. They might also mention an upcoming sale. You should do and say almost anything you can *honestly* and *ethically* to heighten the customer's curiosity and desire to return to your store.'

Keith was excited with the steps just described. But John reassured him that with a little patience and practice, he could soon master each step.

He then suggested that Keith choose one step, preferably his weakest, and for the next few days, concentrate on doing that step as effectively as possible. Then choose the next most difficult step, and do the same. He promised Keith that as he rotated his efforts on the various steps, he would eventually master them.

Rule 9
Whenever possible, follow the six steps
to effective customer relations

The six steps to effective customer relations
1. Greet the customer with enthusiasm and a big smile.
2. Develop a rapport with the customer.
3. Determine the customer's need and make that need explicit.
4. Fill the customer's need with your product or service.
5. Ensure customer satisfaction with your product and company.
6. Thank the customer for his business and invite him back. Heighten his wish to return soon.

CHAPTER 10
The Customer's Responsibility

John was very pleased with his company's new direction. After a busy day, on their way out to the car park, John and Jim began talking about the poor service many customers receive from various businesses. John said, 'It's unfortunate that poor customer service has become acceptable generally. So many businesses have very little regard for their customers, though when confronted, they'll claim differently. But as my grandmother used to say, "you can always tell what someone thinks by how he acts". If businesses regard their customers with any degree of respect, it shows in their actions.'

'I'm surprised,' replied Jim, 'that people tolerate this type of treatment. No one is forced to patronise a particular business. I think customers have been given such bad treatment for so long that they've come to accept it as normal. I don't think customers realise how powerful they are. If they were united, there would be no limit to the quality of service they could demand. For example, if tomorrow, every customer demanded good service or they would go to another place of business, companies would change immediately. You'd see the quickest "about face" of businesses' attitudes towards customer service you've ever seen.'

'It's rather hypocritical on the part of the customers,' added John. 'They complain about poor service and not being treated with respect and courtesy, yet they still patronise the company that treats them that way.'

'I agree,' said Jim, 'but I also think it's necessary for customers to be informed and educated about what they realistically can expect from a business. If customers would take the time and effort to find out what kind of service they could expect, they'd be in a much better position to demand better service when they didn't get it.' Laughing, he continued, 'Listen to me. I'm talking about "they" as though it were other people. I'm one of them. It takes effort to go out of our way when service isn't satisfactory. And yet it wouldn't take long to change the problems with service if everyone did the same thing.'

'Without a doubt,' added John, 'it's the responsibility of a business to treat customers properly. Don't misunderstand me about that. But I've noticed that as a customer, I can do a lot to facilitate better treatment from business.

'I've been into a shop and been the one who was positive and enthusiastic. I've been the one to introduce myself to the assistant and ask his name. I've used his name often during our interaction. It seems to break down the "shield" many employees feel they have – a shield of "acting in the name of the business" with no personal ownership of their actions. But when they hear their name several times, they feel *personally responsible* to do their very best. You see, the assistant's integrity, as well as his responsibility to his company, comes into play, thus increasing the quality of his service. It's more unlikely that an employee will be uncaring, rude or inconsiderate if you use his name several times during the interaction.'

'You've got a good point,' said Jim. 'I think if you pushed that a bit further and treated the assistant as though he were your friend, he would be more likely to go out of his way to make you satisfied.'

'You're probably right. I'm sure you'd be surprised at the quality of service you'd receive. If we, as customers, were cordial to the employees who are helping us, they would be more likely to respond in a similar manner. Let's face it, if a customer is rude, or obnoxious to the assistant, the assistant's typical, though not correct, response is to give that customer *minimal* service and by no means go out of his way to satisfy that customer.

'Wouldn't it be good if more customers would calmly inform management when they receive unsatisfactory service. I know it's management's responsibility to initiate the feedback. But this gets back to having the customers become a more powerful and influential part of turning this customer relations problem around. I think most managers would greatly appreciate a customer who took the time to do that. I will point out that it is equally important to compliment management when they have received good service. We both know that positive reinforcement goes a long way.'

'It's a little frustrating,' said John, 'to see so many businesses floundering. I can't help but think that if they concentrated more on serving their customers effectively many of their problems would disappear. Look at how our company has changed since we implemented our training programme. Somehow, businessmen need to wake up.'

Rule 10
As a customer, expect and demand good service

Important points
1. Never patronise a business that treats customers poorly. If you do, you only reinforce that behaviour.
2. Be an informed and educated customer, then accept nothing short of what you deserve.
3. To get better service as a customer:
   (a) introduce yourself and get the name of the person serving you
   (b) use his name often during the transaction
   (c) be very friendly, positive, and enthusiastic.
4. If you receive bad service, tactfully make management aware of the problem. Likewise, if you receive exceptionally good service, make management aware of your pleasant experience.

CHAPTER 11
The Challenge

After inaugurating a concentrated effort to make every customer satisfied, sales began to increase. John developed a larger and more loyal customer base. And in less than a year, his business was once again profitable.

He gained a reputation for knowing how to treat customers like Royalty. He became a strong advocate for effective customer relations. His counsel was sought by many 'floundering' businessmen and he became a very popular speaker.

On one occasion, John was to address a large group of entrepreneurs. After his introduction, John stood at the podium for several minutes in silence. The audience became restless, wondering what the problem might be. He then said 'I regretfully remind you of a sad tale. We were once the industrial giant of the world. With that leadership came great economic power in world markets. The industrial age has come and gone, as has our dominance and its accompanying power.

'Today we have a great new opportunity. I'm referring to the area of customer relations. Tomorrow, this area will be the battlefield of rival companies.

'Products and services offered by rival companies have become very similar in features and price. Competition in many industries has forced prices down to precarious levels – levels that are forcing some companies into bankruptcy. In the future, the greatest opportunity for profitability, and in most cases mere survival, lies in the area of customer relations.

'There is a new sector in the economy experiencing tremendous growth, the service sector. I've often thought it a paradox that we call this new sector the "service" sector. What has the word service come to mean? Today, there appears to be a one-dimensional definition, that of "not manufacturing." But what happened to the notion of service, meaning to *serve* the customer? Effective customer service should be the essence of the service sector, not just a lame namesake. Effective customer relations should permeate each organisation, be it profit, non-profit, educational, religious, manufacturing, and yes, even service.

'Small businesses are playing an increasingly important role in our community. These small businesses have typically relied on unparalleled customer service for survival and profitability. I'm not quite sure what they are relying on today, but it's not customer relations.

'In general, customer service in this country is terrible. We've got to wake up! Today is the day to prepare for tomorrow's battles. It is *critical* that we do an "about face" in the area of customer relations. If we, the business owners and managers don't act immediately, the customers will *demand* changes. Whether from their collective action or from overseas competition, major changes in the area of customer relations are imminent. If either the customer, or your competition, is the impetus for change, it will be more difficult and costly to bring about that change. Changes will be smoother and more profitable if you take the *first* step rather than being forced to react at the last minute. Battles are won because of *action*, not reaction.

'Before we are again brought to our knees by the competition abroad, let's take a good, hard look at the area of customer relations in our respective businesses. Let's do what we can to cure this cancer of poor customer service. Tremendous customer service will be your key to success in future years. It is not an added cost or an extra expense, it's an investment in future survival and prosperity.

'Together let's raise the standard of service to our customers from deplorable to phenomenal, and in so doing become a world leader in customer relations.

'My challenge to all of you is simple. *Treat each and every customer like Royalty!* For it will be your "golden link" to more customers, increased sales, and greater profitability.

'The word is *excellence*, the area is *customer relations*, and the time is *NOW*! The choice, my friends, is up to *you*!'

The group exploded into thunderous applause and gave him a standing ovation. The audience knew the truth had been spoken and they were excited to accept his challenge. They sensed the greatness of this man who was well acquainted with the heights and depths of success and failure – especially one very special person who sat in the front row, his wife Judy. Here she was supporting him the best way she could. She knew what he had gone through to rise once again to prominence in the business community.

After dinner at their favourite restaurant, John and his wife talked about their experiences over the past year. John said there were several reasons why he was able to pull his business from near bankruptcy back to a thriving business. But one reason had by far the greatest impact – a continuous training programme for all of his employees on the ten steps to dynamic customer relations. Under his leadership, they'd made their customers 'kings' once again and regained the loyal customer base they had previously enjoyed.

'Effective customer relations,' John said, 'is no longer just a part of our business, it's now the heart of our business, and the central focus of all our planning and training. We've learned our lesson well – we'll never again forget who really is our boss, pays our salaries, and controls our business. We'll make sure our customers receive our very best!'

Summary

Ten rules to effective customer relations

1. Never overlook or underestimate the importance of effective customer relations.
2. The customer is always right.
3. Always be positive and enthusiastic.
4. Communication must be open, honest, and prompt.
5. A customer is satisfied when his need has been filled or his problem solved courteously and promptly.
6. A customer is loyal when, over time, he has received consistent, prompt, and courteous service and products.
7. Treat each customer like Royalty.
8. Management is ultimately responsible for effective and efficient customer relations.
9. Whenever possible, follow the six steps to effective customer relations.
10. As a customer, expect and demand good service.

Further Reading from Kogan Page

Customer Service: How to Achieve Total Customer Satisfaction, Malcolm
  Peel

Better management skills

Effective Meeting Skills: How to Make Meetings More Productive, Marion E
  Haynes
Effective Performance Appraisals, Robert B Maddux
Effective Presentation Skills, Steve Mandel
The Fifty-Minute Supervisor: A Guide for the Newly Promoted, Elwood N
  Chapman
How to Develop a Positive Attitude, Elwood N Chapman
Make Every Minute Count: How to Manage Your Time Effectively, Marion
  E Haynes
Successful Negotiation, Robert B Maddux
Team Building: An Exercise in Leadership, Robert B Maddux